Weaning

Introduction

As parents, we want only the best for our children and what better start in life can we give them than the foods that we offer? Those first mini-spoonfuls of ultra-smooth baby purée mark the start of a new and exciting stage in a baby's development. At the beginning, we need to teach a baby to sip and swallow rather than to suck. This is a quite different reflex and one that takes time to learn; it is only once this has been mastered that food can become important nutritionally.

Right: Encourage your baby to feed herself as soon as she is keen to try. The more she practises, the better her coordination will be.

We are all aware of the importance of a healthy diet, but the balance of a baby's diet is different from that of an adult. Foods need to be nutrient-dense because, although appetites are small, growth rate is enormous. At the same time, foods need to be easy to digest.

- **Fat** is important for energy and is most readily absorbed from full-fat dairy foods, such as milk, yoghurt and cheese.
- **Fibre** – although important to an adult's diet – should be kept to a minimum, especially for very young children. Getting the balance and range of foods right in the early months can help to prevent obesity, heart disease, diabetes and osteoporosis later on, and may even increase your child's IQ.

Just as there are critical periods for learning to walk, speak and recognize people, so there seems to be a critical period for the development of taste preferences. The foundations for adult food preferences are laid during a child's first 2 years and many children find it hard to accept foods that were not offered during this crucial period.

This book is packed with practical advice and helpful tips that cover everything you need to know when feeding your baby during the first year. Our simple at-a-glance charts show you exactly which food to introduce and when, and which foods to keep off the menu at every step. Ideas and tips are given for everything from first baby purées to more adventurous meals and the joys of sharing family meals as your baby approaches his first birthday. There is no greater way of showing our children how much we care than by the foods we offer them.

Did you know?

Family values, traditions and culture also influence the types of food that we eat. The senses of taste and smell develop in a baby 28 weeks into pregnancy, which means that an unborn child becomes familiar with the flavour palette of its culture even before birth.

from breast to bottle

- Milk: the perfect first food

- Moving from breast to bottle

- Which formula milk should you use?

- How much formula milk should you give?

1

- Your baby's growth chart

- Safety

- Sterilizing equipment

- Introducing other drinks

- Moving from bottle to beaker and cup

Milk: the perfect first food

In the early months, the only food that a baby requires to meet her nutritional needs is milk – either breast or formula. All babies are born with a natural store of iron to last them for the first 6 months and this is supplemented to some extent by the milk.

Above: Make sure that you are comfortable when breastfeeding, with your baby at the correct height so that she can 'latch on' easily.

Breast milk

Breast milk gives your baby the very best start in life. It contains all the nutrients that she needs in exactly the right proportions and provides many antibodies to help fight infections, as well as hormones and other growth-promoting factors. The high levels of fatty acids in breast milk also protect babies who are susceptible to allergies (those born into families with a history of food intolerance or allergies, such as asthma or eczema). Levels of iron in breast milk are low but the iron is in a readily absorbed form and combines with your baby's own iron store. In addition, the composition of breast milk adjusts if your baby is premature and adapts as she grows and her needs change – it will even become more dilute in hot weather to satisfy your baby's thirst. Moreover, it is sterile, free and always ready at the right temperature, virtually on demand.

Breastfeeding

Breastfeeding, like any new skill, can be difficult to master, especially in the early days. Give yourself time, get plenty of rest and be sure to drink plenty of water. How your baby latches on to the breast is crucial and can be painful if not done correctly. Persevere and do not be afraid to seek advice from your midwife (up to 10 days after the birth) and health visitor (from 10 days after the birth), or from a breastfeeding counsellor via your local health

centre or parenting group. Breastfeed for as long
as you and your baby are happy to do so – be it
for 6 weeks, 6 months, a year or longer.

Plus points
Breastfeeding has many advantages for your baby.
- Breast milk changes to meet your baby's needs.
- A breast feed will provide your baby with the
  equivalent of a two-course meal, rather like a
  starter and a main course, with the foremilk that
  comes first quenching thirst and the hindmilk that
  follows satisfying hunger.
- Breast milk is easy to digest, with little if any
  waste products. This is why breastfed babies
  hardly ever smell unpleasant.
- The more your baby feeds, the more milk your
  body will produce.
- Vital antibodies in breast milk help to fight
  infection and give protection for as long as you
  breastfeed, allowing your baby's immune system
  time to develop.
- A completely breastfed baby is less likely to
  develop allergies, such as asthma and eczema.

Breastfeeding is also good for you
- It helps you regain your figure quickly after birth.
- Women who breastfeed may have a lower risk of
  developing ovarian cancer and pre-menopausal
  breast cancer.
- It is inexpensive – forget about bottles, teats,
  formula milk and sterilizing units. All you need
  is a couple of good nursing bras.
- Breast milk is always ready and at the right
  temperature, cutting down on stress.

Below: Breastfeed for as long as you
and your baby are happy to do so.

Moving from breast to bottle

The introduction of a bottle doesn't necessarily mean the end of breastfeeding. Many women express milk successfully and are able to continue with breastfeeds, even if they are not there for the occasional afternooon, or while at work.

Above: Formula milk is designed to resemble breast milk as closely as possible.

If you are breastfeeding, you can introduce breast milk from a bottle as soon as you are able to express enough. But many mothers prefer to do this once feeding is well established.

- Introduce a bottle to your child once a day, for just a few minutes.
- Offer the bottle with breast milk, formula or a little cooled boiled water (see page 20), but keep the amounts of water low if you wish to continue with breastfeeding.
- Give the bottle before your baby is really hungry.
- Get your partner or a friend to offer the bottle so that your baby cannot smell your breast milk, or offer the bottle to your baby while he is sitting in a baby-chair.
- Try softening the teat in boiling water before use – but remember to allow it to cool before giving it to your baby!
- Gently brush the bottle teat against your baby's lips and let him reach for it.
- Start small – your baby may only take 25ml (1fl oz) at first, so offer tiny amounts of expressed milk or prepared formula and make sure you throw away the leftovers. Do not be tempted to reheat them for later use.
- Experiment with styles of teat – some babies prefer a softer latex teat rather than one made from silicone.
- Check that the teat has the right size of hole for your baby. If the hole is too small, your baby will

Remember!

Bottle-feeding will give your partner a chance to help out, making him feel involved and giving you some time off.

have to suck hard and may become cross. If it is too large, the milk flow will be too fast and he may gag. Check the packaging – manufacturers suggest suitable age ranges.

Bottle-feeding

Everyone knows that Breast is Best, but it is only best if you and your baby feel comfortable together doing it. Some mothers know that they will bottle-feed from the start while others come to it after a few weeks or months of painful breastfeeding.

Formula milk is designed to mimic breast milk as closely as possible and it is just as nutritious. However, it takes longer to digest than breast milk, so you may find that bottle-fed babies fall into a 4-hourly routine early on. Remember that all babies are different, so follow your baby's lead.

Read the instructions

Do not be tempted to round-up the formula scoop or to pack down the powder too densely. If the milk is made up too strongly, far from being good for your baby it will be too concentrated, difficult to digest, and it will make his kidneys work harder.

Below: Choose the method of feeding that makes you both feel most relaxed. Breastfeeding is not right for all mums.

Which formula milk to use?

Formula milks are based on cow's milk, but have been modified and carefully formulated to give your baby the right balance of nutrients. Once you have found a brand that your baby likes, stay with it, because it can be unsettling for her if you keep changing.

Remember!

Do not give a baby unmodified soya milk or fresh pasteurized goat's milk because these milks lack vital vitamins and minerals.

Above: Follow the milk formula manufacturer's directions carefully.

Formula milk comes in a number of different forms.

- **Infant formula.** There are two types of infant formula. The first, suitable straight from birth, has 60 per cent whey and 40 per cent curds, plus added long-chain polyunsaturated fatty acids (naturally present in breast milk and important for the development of the brain, eye and nervous system). The second, intended for hungrier babies, has 20 per cent whey and 80 per cent curds, which take longer to digest so that the baby feels full for longer.
- **Follow-on formula.** Suitable for babies from 6 months, this contains 20 per cent whey and 80 per cent curds, plus added iron, calcium, zinc and vitamin D to meet the older baby's increased nutritional needs.
- **Soya-based formula.** This is suitable for a baby with cow's milk intolerance or for a mother who cannot breastfeed but wants to bring up her baby on a vegan diet. Such formulas do not contain the milk sugar lactose but are sweetened with glucose syrup. They are not suitable for premature babies or babies with kidney problems because they contain traces of aluminium. Nor are they suitable for babies with a family history of allergy to soya products. Only give this formula after getting specialist medical advice.
- **Goat's milk infant formula.** This can be less allergenic than cow's milk because, unlike cow's milk, it does not contain the enzyme gamma-

casein. It also forms smaller curds in the stomach and so is easier for the baby to digest. Do not give it to your baby unless you are following specialist medical advice.

What about cow's milk?

Full-fat pasteurized cow's milk may be mixed with your baby's cereals or cooked food from the age of 6 months, but it is not recommended as a main drink before the age of 1 year. Cow's milk is low in iron and other nutrients needed for growth, unlike formula milk, which is fortified with iron and vitamins. The same applies to goat's, sheep's, soya (non-infant carton), rice and oat milks.

Because full-fat milk contains more fat-soluble vitamins and energy, most nutritionists would prefer children to be offered full-fat milk unless they have a weight problem. However, you may offer semi-skimmed cow's milk when your child is over 2 years old and skimmed milk if she is over 5 years old, but only if she has a good appetite and eats a mixed and varied diet.

Cow's milk intolerance

Fewer than one in fifty young children have an allergy to cow's milk. If you are worried that your child might be one of them, talk to your doctor, who may refer you to a State Registered paediatric dietician. Do not make any changes without advice because excluding milk from your child's diet could affect her growth.

How much formula milk should you give?

From the age of 4 months, or once weaning has begun, you should allow about 60ml (2.5fl oz) formula milk per 450g (16oz) of your baby's bodyweight a day.

How much milk?

• **4–6 months**
600ml (20fl oz/1 pint) breast milk or infant formula.

• **6–9 months**
500–600ml (17–20fl oz/ 1 pint) breast milk, formula or follow-on milk, plus small amounts of wholemilk in cooking or breakfast cereals.

• **9–12 months**
500–600ml (17–20fl oz/ 1 pint) breast milk, formula or follow-on milk, plus larger amounts of wholemilk in cooking or breakfast cereals.

• **From 1 year**
Minimum 600ml (20fl oz/ 1 pint) or 350ml (12fl oz) wholemilk, plus two small servings of dairy produce in cooking.

Can you give a baby too much?

Most babies will regulate their feeding and stop sucking when they have had enough. A few babies will cry at the end of a feed, but you should check that your baby is winded before refilling the bottle too quickly. Too much milk, drunk too quickly, may make your baby sick. A very hungry baby may benefit from a larger feed in the evening to help satisfy him through the night.

If you offer a top-up bottle but find that your baby only takes 25ml (1fl oz), it is possible that he would have been just as happy with a dummy for comfort. Be guided by your baby: if he is happy and contented, carry on as you are. Discuss any fears you have with your health visitor, who will have been monitoring your baby's weight gain and will know you and your baby well.

Right: A well-fed baby will be happy and contented.

Your baby's growth chart

Regular weight checks at your local health centre are a good way of picking up on any health or developmental problems at an early stage, and are an ideal opportunity for you to discuss any concerns with your health visitor.

Left: All babies have their own pattern of growth and development.

Your baby's weight will be recorded at the health centre by your health visitor. The centile chart is drawn up by plotting the weights on a graph-like chart (see right) and can be a good indication that your baby is feeding and developing well. In the first 6 months, your baby should put on 100–225g (4–8oz) each week, doubling his birthweight by the age of 5–6 months. In the second 6 months, weight gain slows to about 75–150g (3–5oz) each week.

Growth charts

Growth charts were originally based on a sample of babies who were predominantly bottle-fed. It is now recognized that breastfed babies grow at different rates, so a second chart has been introduced. Generally, breastfed babies put on more weight initially than bottle-fed babies, but then become leaner and lighter at around 3 months. Some even show a dip in weight gain.

Ask your health visitor for the chart that is right for you and your baby, and discuss any worries that you may have about feeding. All babies are individuals with their own pattern of growth and development. The only cause for concern is any excessive weight gain or weight loss. It is interesting to note that length and head circumference (indicating brain growth) should develop at the same rate for both bottle-fed babies and breastfed babies.

Safety

Warm milk makes an ideal breeding ground for the bacteria that cause stomach upsets, so you should take every precaution.

tip

Cool-bags can be used to store night-time feeds in the bedroom and you can save a trip to the kitchen by warming the feed in a plug-in bottle-warmer by the bed.

Above: Cartons of ready-to-use formula milk and a sterilized bottle make a great standby when you are going out.

1 Wash and sterilize all equipment (see opposite) until your baby is 6 months old, and bottles and teats for as long as they are used.

2 Clean all traces of milk from used teats with a bottlebrush and hot, soapy water. Rinse well and sterilize before re-use.

3 If you are making up several bottles, transfer them to the main part of the fridge (not the shelf in the door) immediately afterwards and use them within 24 hours.

4 Warm a bottle of milk in hot water or a bottle-warmer. A microwave oven can heat unevenly and may produce hot-spots, so if you use one shake the bottle thoroughly before use.

5 Always check the temperature of the milk by putting a few drops on the inside of your wrist – it should be the same temperature as your skin – before offering it to your baby.

6 Once you have warmed a bottle, do not leave it lying around. Offer it to your baby as soon as it is cool enough to drink.

7 Throw away leftover milk after a feed – do not be tempted to reheat it.

8 When going out for the day, transport made-up bottles in a small, well-insulated cool-bag with a frozen ice-block and use within 3 hours.

Sterilizing equipment

Hygiene is paramount when preparing food for your baby, since their immature immune systems make them much more susceptible to food poisoning and other bugs.

There are a number of different types of sterilizer available on the market.

- **Steam sterilizer.** This free-standing electric machine is available in two sizes and takes about 10 minutes plus a short standing time. It is good for bottles, teats and feeding spoons.
- **Microwave unit.** A small, compact plastic container that fits inside the microwave, this takes about 7 minutes on full power. It is ideal for bottles, teats and feeding spoons, and handy when staying overnight with friends or family.
- **Cold-water sterilizer.** This is a more old-fashioned but economical method, in which items are submerged in sterilizing solution diluted with water for 30 minutes. It is good for bottles, teats and larger items.

Submerge items that will not fit into a sterilizing unit, such as ice-cube trays or feeding bowls, in a large saucepan of water and boil them for 5 minutes. Wash liquidizer or food-processor bowls, plastic chopping boards or knives in a dishwasher, or wash them conventionally then rinse them with boiling water from the kettle and let them drip dry.

Above: An electric steam sterilizer is the easiest and most popular method with new mums.

Introducing other drinks

It is vitally important to offer your baby drinks that are suitable for his age, and not those geared to older children or adults.

Above: *Choose from a wide range of brightly coloured, different-sized trainer beakers, from your local supermarket or chemist.*

Remember!

Water, including bottled still water, must be boiled and cooled for all babies up to 6 months of age.

Cooled boiled water can be introduced to formula-fed babies from about the age of 6 weeks, while breastfed babies do not need anything else to drink. Breast milk has the amazing ability to change naturally and become more thirst-quenching but, for a mother who feels that her baby is constantly on the breast, offering a bottle of cooled boiled water can provide a welcome breathing space. Also, if you are planning to go back to work, it can be helpful to get your baby used to the idea of a teat in readiness for formula feeds. If you are breastfeeding, it is best to wait until your baby is 3–4 months old before introducing him to the bottle.

Water

- Your baby may be more receptive to the idea of drinking water if it is just warm rather than cold.
- Do not be tempted to add flavourings or sweeteners to water – a thirsty baby will happily drink it in its natural state.
- Tap water should be boiled and cooled before use, using water that has been freshly drawn from the tap. Repeatedly boiling water will increase the levels of sodium in it, which could be dangerous for your baby.
- Do not give your baby any form of artificially softened water, for example, from a mains tap fitted with a water softener.
- Filtered water from a jug-style water filter can be given, but change the filters regularly.
- Never give sparkling mineral water or water with a high natural mineral content (often known as 'natural mineral water') to a baby under 2 years

old. Make sure that you read the label very carefully, and only use bottled water with a sodium content under 10mg per 100ml.

Fruit juices

Well-diluted, unsweetened fruit juices, such as apple or orange, can be gradually introduced as a drink from 9 months of age, provided that there is no history of allergies – orange juice can cause a reaction in some children. If you are at all concerned, talk to your health visitor or doctor.

Fruit juices naturally contain fruit sugars and acids, which help to make the juice taste good, and are best offered at mealtimes because the saliva created by eating helps to neutralize these sugars and acids. Research has shown that it is not only what is drunk that is crucial, but also how it is drunk. Prolonged sucking of fruit juice and squashes from a bottle can cause dental erosion because the fruit juice stays in the mouth far longer.

Encourage your child to drink water or milk between meals or, if you do offer fruit juice, serve it with a few squares of Cheddar cheese to neutralize the fruit sugars and acids.

Read the labels

Get into the habit of reading labels because not all drinks are what they appear – some fruit drinks may contain as little as 5 per cent fruit juice.

- Look at where sugar appears in the list of ingredients: the nearer it is to the beginning of the list, the higher the amount. It may be included in different forms and be listed as maltose, maltodextrin, sucrose, fructose, glucose, glucose or corn syrup – it may appear several times on a list of ingredients but under different names.
- Avoid fruit juices, cordials and squashes that contain artificial sweeteners, such as aspartame, saccharine or acesulfame-K. These can act as a brain stimulant and are not intended for babies.

Remember!

For children under 1 year old, dilute cartons of fresh orange or apple juice in the ratio 1 part fruit juice to 10 parts water and serve in a cup or beaker at mealtimes.

Did you know?

Seventy-five per cent of the weight of a newborn baby is made up of water.

Moving from bottle to beaker and cup

As your baby grows up, try to introduce a feeder beaker before she becomes too dependent on feeding from the bottle, and reluctant to try anything new.

Remember!

Always supervise a small child who is drinking or eating and never give a bottle to a baby in a cot.

Start to offer a soft-spouted feeding beaker at mealtimes from the age of 5–6 months, although, in the early days, your baby will need your help to hold the beaker (see Tip, opposite). Most babies begin to master the idea between 6 and 8 months of age, although the majority will be unable to hold an unlidded cup until after their first birthday. Playing with a cup in the bath can help their coordination and a cup with handles makes life much easier. Ideally, aim to stop using a bottle by the time your baby is 1 year old.

Most babies are happy to use a beaker at mealtimes but many are reluctant to give up the breast or bottle as a comfort feed night and morning. Once your baby is eating three meals a day, you will probably be able to cut out the morning bottle feed or breast feed, although the night-time feed may be trickier!

Left: *For a young child just learning to hold a beaker, it can be fun to offer one in the bath – but don't let him drink the bath water!*

'My baby has gone off milk'

This is not uncommon when a beaker has been introduced. Some babies associate a bottle with comfort and, once a beaker is introduced, they are not so keen to drink milk in this new way. Providing that your baby is drinking plenty of fluid and eating well, there is no need to panic. As she begins to eat more solid food, her milk consumption will naturally tail off.

Ideally your baby should still be drinking about 500–600ml (17–20fl oz/1 pint) of follow-on formula milk a day, between 6 and 12 months. If she is drinking less than this, encourage her to eat more yoghurt, fromage frais, grated cheese and milk in savoury sauces or soups, with breakfast cereal, or frozen as lollies.

As a rough guide 200ml (7fl oz) full-fat or formula milk is equivalent to 40g (1½oz) Cheddar cheese or 150g (5oz) yoghurt.

tip

Learning to coordinate hand-to-mouth movements can be tricky and frustrating for a fiercely independent child. Fill a cup with only a little cooled boiled water at first, to ensure that she will not make a mess if she tilts it, or drops its contents over herself or onto the floor.

Is it wrong to give a baby weak tea or coffee?

Tea and coffee, however weak, reduce the absorption of iron and other minerals from food, while the caffeine present acts as a stimulant. They are not recommended for young children, even if served without sugar and with a lot of milk.

first mini-mouthfuls

- When milk is not enough

- The importance of age

- Introducing solid foods

- Slowly does it

- What else can you give your baby?

2

- Food allergies

- Do not leave it too late

- Feeding plan: getting started

- Foods to avoid

- What to introduce and when

When milk is not enough

As your baby grows, a diet of milk alone will not be enough to sustain him. Most babies will need extra nourishment from around 4–6 months old, although some may be in less of a hurry.

Above: *The baby who is constantly chewing his fist may be trying to tell you that he is hungry.*

By the time your baby is 5–6 months old, he will have doubled his birthweight and by 12 months he may have trebled it. While breast milk or formula milk has been providing all his nutritional needs in the early months, his rapid growth and development will soon require more nutrients than milk alone can provide.

By the time your baby has reached 4–6 months of age, you may begin to notice that he:

- Seems hungry and wants a feed, even though he has been happily in a routine of four or five full feeds from both breasts or a 250ml (8fl oz) formula feed at even 3½–4-hourly intervals.
- Still seems hungry after a feed from both breasts or a 250ml (8fl oz) formula feed.
- Wakes up increasingly earlier, or wakes in the night whereas he had been sleeping through.
- Is beginning to chew his hands excessively and keeps trying to put things into his mouth.

What is weaning?

Weaning is the gradual move by your baby from milk feeds to ultra-smooth food purées, then to coarser purées, until he is fully joining in with family meals at around 12 months of age.

How will you know when your baby is ready?

At 6 months or before, your baby will start to:

- Seem generally restless and grizzly.
- Look longingly at what you are eating.
- Show the other signs listed above.

The importance of age

Official UK government guidelines recommend that babies should be exclusively breastfed until 6 months, but if parents choose to wean earlier than this, solid food should not be introduced before 17 weeks.

A report by the Committee on Medical Aspects of Food Policy (the COMA report) entitled *Weaning and the Weaning Diet*, advises that introducing solids too early or increasing amounts too quickly could affect babies in the following ways.

1 **Damage to the digestive system.** The development of a baby's gut lining and the set of enzymes required for digestion takes up to 4 months. Until this age, the kidneys are not mature enough to cope with solid food waste products.

2 **Choking.** Until 4 months, neuromuscular coordination is not sufficiently developed to enable a baby to control his head and neck movement while sitting upright, supported in a chair. Therefore, he may not be able to swallow food easily by moving it from the front of his mouth to the back, which involves a different set of reflexes from drinking milk.

3 **Increased risk of allergies.** Asthma, eczema, hay fever, and gluten (coeliac disease) and peanut allergies, for example, are more likely to develop, especially if there is a family history of allergies.

4 **Cough.** Scottish research has linked weaning at 4 months with a persistent cough.

5 **Obesity.** Research has linked overfeeding in early weaning to obesity and an increased risk of cancer, diabetes and heart disease in later life.

Allergies

If you have a family history of food allergies, asthma, or eczema, it may be advisable to delay weaning. Ask your doctor or health visitor for more information.

Remember!

The introduction of those first mini-mouthfuls of baby purée is a huge milestone in your baby's development and consequently what you offer is vitally important.

Introducing solid foods

Although your baby will have been fed on demand until now, it is important that the introduction of solid foods is more structured. Begin with just one mini-meal mid-morning, then gradually introduce a second mini-meal after 2–3 weeks. A third meal can then be introduced a further 2–3 weeks after that.

Above: Storing frozen cubes of baby food saves time and washing-up.

Once three meals are on the menu, try to space them out evenly, bringing them nearer to the family's breakfast, lunch and supper times.

First on the menu

The easiest and most comforting first food is baby rice. Sold in powdered form, this is quick and easy to prepare and, because portion size is so tiny at this stage, it is much the most convenient. Mix 1 teaspoonful of powdered rice with expressed breast milk, made-up formula milk or cooled boiled water, according to the instructions, until it is a smooth, slightly sloppy purée. The taste and texture are not dissimilar to milk, so most babies are happy to tuck in. If your baby seems at all distressed by this first taste of solids, take the food away and try again after a few days.

Continue with just one mini-meal over the next 5–7 days, gradually increasing the amount of rice powder from 1 to 3 teaspoonfuls. Do not be tempted to increase the amounts too quickly, especially during the first day or two, because your baby's digestive system needs time to adjust.

As your baby's appetite begins to grow, you may prefer to make your own rice purée with risotto or pudding rice, simmered in formula milk and then puréed and sieved. This can be frozen in sections of an ice-cube tray, but it will need to be thinned with formula milk or cooled boiled water just before serving because the rice swells with standing. Cooked potato or yam can also be offered as a first food and can be cooked in much the same way as you would the rice and, again, served as an ultra-smooth and soft purée.

Remember!

To start with, your baby may only eat 1 teaspoonful of ultra-smooth, slightly sloppy purée, gradually building up to 3 teaspoonfuls after 5–7 days. At this stage, the aim is to introduce your baby to the tastes and texture of this new way of eating, and not for these foods to provide a lot of extra nourishment. That will come later.

Left: Choose a soft plastic baby spoon and small non-breakable plates and bowls for first solid food meals.

Remember!

Within 6–9 weeks your baby
will have progressed from
1–2 teaspoonfuls of baby rice
once a day to three mixed
mini-meals a day.

Basic equipment

Your baby will have such a small appetite at this
stage that it is best to keep feeding bowls small.
Some bowls have easy-to-hold lips around the edge,
or you may prefer to use the top of a sterilized
bottle as a mini-mixing bowl during the first few
days. Choose tiny, specialist, soft-edged weaning
spoons and small bowls for easy feeding.

Feeling secure

Both you and your baby should feel happy and
relaxed when you begin weaning, so you may
prefer to sit her on your lap and drape her and your
clothes with a muslin or clean tea towel. If you think
your baby will be too wriggly, then use the baby-
seat from your car instead. Most babies are unable
to sit in a highchair, even with a headrest, until they
are 6 months old.

When should you introduce the first meal

Most parents find a baby is more receptive to trying
her first solid food after her morning sleep. If you
have other, older children, this means that you will
have completed the school run and will still have
time to feed your baby before you need to do any
lunchtime pick-ups.

Offer your baby just a small milk feed or a feed
from one breast to take the edge off her appetite –
a baby desperate for food will not be easily
persuaded to try a spoon for the first time. Half-fill a
small, soft-edged baby spoon and offer it to your
baby. Do not worry if most of the food appears to
dribble back out of her mouth. Taking food off a
spoon involves quite a different reflex from sucking
and it will take a little time to master. Encourage
your baby with face-to-face interaction and reassure
her with smiles and loving sounds so that this can
be a pleasurable experience.

*Above: In the early days you may
find it easier to feed your baby while
he sits in his car seat.*

Left: *Taking food off a spoon involves quite a different reflex from sucking.*

Below: *Help your baby to use a spoon, by giving her one to play with.*

What if your baby isn't interested in eating from a spoon?

If your baby is less than 6 months old, gaining weight well and sleeping through the night, but shows no interest in solid foods, she may simply not be ready to be weaned. Ask your health visitor or doctor for advice.

For other babies, the problem may be either the idea of the spoon or what is on the spoon. Try again with a different spoon: some have very small bowls and are made of thin, soft plastic while others have soft, almost pliable edges. You could also vary what is on the spoon: try a thin potato purée or, if that meets with rejection, offer a tiny taste of butternut squash purée. Never force-feed a baby and never be tempted to add baby rice to a baby's bottle.

Slowly does it

As always, be guided by your baby and increase the amount of food and number of meals as he is ready – he will soon show you when he has had enough.

Until he is 6 months old, your baby's nutritional needs can still be met from breast milk or formula milk feeds, backed up with his natural body store of iron. Infants who are weaned at 6 months may need to be moved onto a mixed diet more quickly than those who start earlier, and there is no need to purée their food. The first few weeks of weaning are a time of introduction, an opportunity for your baby to adjust to a new style of eating, so do not worry if your baby seems to spit out as much as goes into his mouth. Solid food should be offered in tiny amounts, with just one meal a day at first.

Gradually increase the amount that you offer at this meal over the forthcoming days and, about 14 days after your baby's first meal, offering a second meal as well. By the time that your baby has adjusted to this new style of eating, he will have used up his natural body supply of iron. This will coincide with the larger meals that will meet his increased nutritional needs for growth and development.

Above: *Introduce new flavours by mixing food into a little baby rice, so that they won't taste too strong.*

Right: *Make up baby rice with expressed breast milk, made-up formula milk or cooled boiled water, as the manufacturer directs.*

What else can you give your baby?

At this stage, the foods that you offer should be mild and easy to digest. After all, this is only the beginning. There will be plenty of time to be adventurous later on.

Once your baby is happily tucking into baby rice and potato or yam purée, you could try mixing the rice with a little peeled, cooked and puréed dessert pear or apple. Cook the peeled fruit with a little boiled water and do not be tempted to add any sugar. Ripe pears and dessert apples such as Gala are naturally sweet. Cook them until they are just soft, then purée and sieve them until they absolutely smooth. Stir a teaspoonful of fruit purée into made-up rice for a first taste and then gradually increase the amounts as your baby's appetite grows. Butternut squash or sweet potato also make ideal first foods because they blend to a wonderfully smooth, vibrant orange purée with a delicate taste that babies seem to love.

Once your baby has tried and liked these new flavours, gradually introduce him to parsnip, carrot or courgette purée. These should be peeled (courgettes being the exception) and either cooked in a little boiled water or steamed for several minutes. Adjust the texture after puréeing if necessary, by adding some of the cooking liquid or, if the vegetables were steamed, a little cooled boiled water, expressed milk or formula milk to thin.

What is best: boiling or steaming?

Some water-soluble vitamins and minerals leach out into the cooking water when they are boiled. Providing that you use the minimum amount of water and use the same water when puréeing the foods, they are as good nutritionally as steamed foods. While steamed foods do not lose vitamins and minerals into the cooking water, they will need puréeing with boiled water, expressed milk or formula milk in order to get the texture right. Tiny amounts can easily be cooked in a microwave oven with 2 tablespoonfuls of boiled water. Cook for 2–3 minutes until tender, then purée.

Food allergies

Some children are more likely than others to have an allergic reaction triggered by a particular food. Those most at risk are babies from families with a history of allergy, such as peanut allergy, asthma, eczema or hay fever. An estimated one in ten children is prone to an allergy. Although many will grow out of it by the time they are 2 years old, others will have a sensitivity to eggs, milk, flour or shellfish for life.

Above: *While milk is regarded as a healthy food, one in fifty children have an allergy to cow's milk.*

Current government guidelines suggest that infants with a strong family history of allergy should be breastfed for at least 6 months, longer if possible, to provide them with protective antibodies (see page 11). A family history of food allergies may double your baby's risk of having an allergy, so seek expert advice from your doctor, who may refer you to a State Registered paediatric dietician. If you think that your baby is reacting to a certain food – with griping pains, diarrhoea or frequent posseting after eating – even though you have no family history of allergy, trust your instinct and ask your doctor for advice or insist on a referral to a paediatric dietician. Do not be tempted to exclude foods without professional advice, because a restricted diet may possibly result in malnutrition.

Trigger foods

Listed on the following three pages are common trigger foods. In addition to these, you should also be wary of sesame seeds and products made from them, soya products and fish, especially shellfish – which should not be given before 12 months.

Right: Be aware that peanuts can cause some of the most serious kinds of allergic reactions in children. Furthermore, the peanuts themselves are often covered with salt, which for babies and children must be very restricted.

Peanuts and other nuts

An allergy to any sort of nut is the most serious kind of allergy. Only women with a history of food allergies, asthma or eczema in themselves, their partners or existing children need to avoid peanuts and peanut products during their pregnancy and when breastfeeding.

Symptoms: Anaphylactic shock, a particularly severe and frightening reaction in which the throat swells and breathing gets difficult.

Foods to avoid: Peanuts, peanut butter and unrefined peanut oil. The oil is the most difficult to detect because it is found in many ready meals and snacks, so always read the packet labels and, if in doubt about anything, do not eat it! Do not offer peanuts in any form to a child under 3 years old if there is a family history of peanut allergy. In any case, whole nuts should never be given to children under 5 years old because of the danger of choking. Although it is usually only the peanut, a ground-grown nut, that causes the reaction, some tree nuts can also cause problems, so ask your doctor or paediatric dietician for advice.

Alternatives: Home-made meals, cakes and biscuits. In this way, you can be sure of the ingredients.

Nuts and allergies

If you have no family history of nut allergy, then finely ground almonds or hazelnuts may be mixed into baby foods from the age of 9–12 months. Finely ground peanuts may be offered from 12 months. Never give whole nuts to children under 5 years of age, because there is a danger of choking.

35

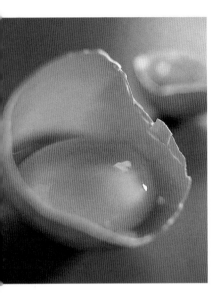

Above: Eggs can aggravate the symptoms of asthma and eczema in child sufferers.

Dairy products

Some children are deficient in lactase, the enzyme needed to digest milk sugar.

Symptoms: Tummy aches and diarrhoea. Consult your doctor if you are worried.

Foods to avoid: Cow's milk, cheese and butter. These should be either limited or omitted completely from the diet.

Alternatives: Soya milk and other soya products. Yoghurt may be tolerated because the bacteria that it contains produce their own lactase. Some babies may also be allergic to cow's milk protein (and soya-based milks) and will require a hypoallergenic milk formula, available on prescription. Do not give unmodified (or carton) soya milks to children who are under 2 years old.

Gluten

This allergy to gluten, a protein found mainly in wheat, is known as coeliac disease.

Symptoms: Diarrhoea and tummy problems, causing damage to the intestine lining and weight loss.

Foods to avoid: Wheat – in forms such as bread, pasta, cakes and flour – barley, rye and oats.

Alternatives: Rice cakes instead of bread, rice or corn noodles instead of wheat pasta, rice or corn (maize) cereals for breakfast, and buckwheat, millet or sorghum flour. Gluten-free bread is available on prescription. If you have a family history of this allergy, your doctor may suggest that you gradually introduce oats, rye and barley from 9 months and wheat from 12 months under close supervision.

Eggs

Symptoms: Rashes or eczema, skin swellings and tummy upsets.

Foods to avoid: Eggs (especially the egg white), cakes, some breads and pastries.

Alternatives: None available.

Tomatoes

Symptoms: Rashes or eczema, and they are linked possibly to hyperactivity.

Foods to avoid: Tomatoes, tomato ketchup, passata, canned tomatoes.

Alternatives: Chopped carrots or red peppers, and ground mild paprika will add colour to dishes. If you have a family history of this allergy, do not introduce tomatoes until your child has reached at least 9 months.

Citrus fruit and strawberries

Symptoms: Rashes or eczema.

Foods to avoid: Fresh oranges, satsumas, orange lollies, fruit yoghurts, squash.

Alternatives: Bananas, pears, plums, apricots, dried fruits, apple juice to drink.

Above: *Tomatoes contain salicylates, which can irritate the stomach and have been linked with hyperactivity.*

Left: *Some children are allergic to strawberries, so watch closely the first few times that you give them to your child.*

Do not leave it too late

Although babies develop at different rates and weaning can be introduced at anytime between 4 and 6 months of age, it is advisable not to leave it too late. After 6 months your baby's natural body store of iron will have been used up and milk alone cannot provide sufficient iron. Also, there is the danger that babies who are introduced to solids later are less likely to be receptive to new flavours, tastes and textures.

Left: From 6 months, your baby's nutritional needs increase and he requires a varied diet as well as milk.

What if your baby will not touch solids?

Babies of 6 months or more may refuse solids if they drink a lot of milk, especially if they are still feeding during the night. If you are worried that your older baby is not taking enough solids, you may need to reduce the amount of milk he drinks. Talk to your health visitor about gradually reducing his milk intake and complementing this with weaning foods. By the end of 6 months, he should be having 600ml (20fl oz/1 pint) breast or formula milk a day, with a little cow's milk in cooked food. Again, talk over any worries with your health visitor or doctor.

What about premature babies?

If your baby was born before 36 weeks, it is important to seek professional advice from your doctor or health visitor. Your baby may have low levels of iron and zinc – these are only laid down during the last few weeks of pregnancy – and he may need to be given vitamin drops as a supplement (see page 76, 'Should you give your child vitamin drops?').

As a general rule, solid foods can be offered from 4 to 6 months after your baby's expected due date.

Below: 4–6 months after your baby's expected due date is the right time to offer solid food.

Feeding plan: getting started

The four easy-to-follow charts below give suggested meal plans for the first 4 weeks of weaning, from 17 weeks.

Remember!

Be guided by your baby – all babies are individuals and develop at different rates. Just because your friend's baby is happily tucking into two solid meals a day it doesn't mean that your baby is ready to start on solids.

Infants who are weaned at 6 months may need to be moved onto a mixed diet more quickly than those who start earlier and their food doesn't need to be puréed (see 6–9 months feeding plan on page 46).

Week 1: one meal a day

Breakfast	Milk feed
Mid-morning	Small milk feed. 1–2 teaspoonfuls of baby rice, mixed according to pack directions.
Lunch	Milk feed
Mid-afternoon	Milk feed
Tea	Milk feed
Bedtime	Milk feed

Week 2: one meal a day

Breakfast	Milk feed
Mid-morning	Small milk feed. 3 teaspoonfuls baby rice, mixed according to pack directions.
Lunch	Milk feed
Mid-afternoon	Milk feed
Tea	Milk feed
Bedtime	Milk feed

Week 3: two meals a day

	Day 1	Day 2	Day 3	Day 4	Day 5
Breakfast	Milk feed	Milk feed	Milk feed	Milk feed	Milk feed
Mid-morning	Potato purée	Apple purée	Butternut squash purée	Parsnip purée	Pear purée
Lunch	Milk feed	Milk feed	Milk feed	Milk feed	Milk feed
Mid-afternoon	Baby rice	Baby rice	Baby rice	Baby rice	Baby rice
Tea	Milk feed	Milk feed	Milk feed	Milk feed	Milk feed
Bedtime	Milk feed	Milk feed	Milk feed	Milk feed	Milk feed

Week 4: two meals a day

	Day 1	Day 2	Day 3	Day 4	Day 5
Breakfast	Milk feed	Milk feed	Milk feed	Milk feed	Milk feed
Mid-morning	Parsnip purée	Butternut squash purée	Sweet potato purée	Sweet potato purée	Carrot purée
Lunch	Milk feed	Milk feed	Milk feed	Milk feed	Milk feed
Mid-afternoon	Apple purée	Pear purée	Pear purée	Apple purée	Apple purée
Tea	Milk feed	Milk feed	Milk feed	Milk feed	Milk feed
Bedtime	Milk feed	Milk feed	Milk feed	Milk feed	Milk feed

Foods to avoid

Your baby's digestive system needs time to adjust from a diet of milk only, so the best thing is not to bombard him with too many flavours, too quickly.

Above: Small amounts of orange juice may be added to meals from 6–9 months and diluted as a drink from 9–12 months, as long as there is no family history of allergies.

If you are going to wean before 6 months, a number of foods must be avoided. All babies under 12 months need to avoid honey, shellfish, salt and sugar.

- **Grains:** such as wheat, oats, barley and rye. The protein found in these grains, known as gluten, can lead to coeliac disease in some susceptible infants, causing damage to the intestine. This mostly runs in families but, because it is difficult to detect in babies, it makes sense not to introduce grains until the intestine is more mature and able to digest this protein.
- **Acidic fruits:** such as citrus fruits, berries and currants, and strong-tasting fruits such as rhubarb, gooseberries and plums. These can be difficult for an immature digestive system to digest and their strong taste can be off-putting for a young baby.
- **Strong spices and flavourings:** such as garlic or other herbs.
- **Salt:** occurs naturally in food, but a baby's kidneys cannot cope with any further doses of salt. Adding it could also lead to a salt preference and high blood pressure later on in life. Avoid stock cubes, yeast extract, canned pulses with added salt, salted or cured bacon or ham, smoked or salted fish and hydrolyzed vegetable protein.
- **Sugar:** choose food that has naturally occurring sugar, so that your baby does not grow up with a sweet tooth or susceptibility to tooth decay.
- **Honey:** this occasionally contains a bacterium that

can cause botulism in babies; avoid giving it before 12 months.

- **Nuts and seeds:** such as peanuts, and tree nuts, such as walnuts, almonds and hazelnuts, as well as sesame seeds, sunflower seeds, can trigger allergies in some children.
- **Cow's, goat's or soya milk:** unless specially modified for babies. Give soya or goat's milk only on the advice of a doctor or specialist.
- **Eggs:** can trigger an allergic reaction. Avoid both egg yolk and egg white at this stage.
- **Offal:** such as cow's, pig's or chicken liver. Avoid because the vitamin A levels that they contain are too high for a tiny baby.
- **Shellfish:** are strong-tasting and a common cause of tummy upsets, so are best avoided until your baby is 12 months old.
- **Foods high in fibre:** such as dried or canned pulses or beans and lentils (red lentils can be introduced in tiny amounts from 5 months). Fibre has too strong a laxative effect and this will prevent the absorption of vital nutrients from the rest of the meal.

Below: It is vitally important to offer your baby food that his digestive system is able to cope with.

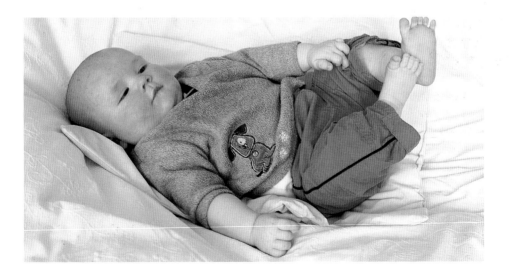

What to introduce and when

This easy-to-use, at-a-glance guide will prove an invaluable check on when to begin broadening your child's diet, from first foods at 4 months and up to your baby's first birthday.

At 4–5 months

Meals per day	One mini-meal moving on to two meals after 2–3 weeks.
Portion size	1–2 teaspoonfuls for first 5–7 days, gradually increasing to 3 teaspoonfuls after 7–10 days.
Texture	Ultra-smooth, slightly sloppy, sieved purée.
Flavours	Mild and bland. Gradually introduce new flavours one at a time, on their own or mixed with baby rice or puréed potato.
Vegetables	Puréed and sieved, steamed or boiled potato, moving on to yam, sweet potato, butternut squash, parsnip or carrot.
Fruit	Peeled dessert pears or apples, cooked with a little boiled water and puréed without sugar and sieved.
Grains and pulses	Non-gluten and low-fibre grains, such as plain powdered baby rice or home-made rice purée with water or formula milk. Cornmeal (not precooked polenta grains), millet, ground sago or tapioca.
Dairy foods	No
Meat	No
Fish	No
Eggs	No
Nuts, seeds	No
Milk	Breast feeds or at least 600ml (20 fl oz/1 pint) formula milk daily.
Drinks	Cooled boiled water.

Left: From 4 months, your baby is ready to try simple flavour combinations.

At 5–6 months

Meals per day	After 6–9 weeks of weaning, introduce a third meal.
Portion size	Gradually increase meal size to 2–3 tablespoonfuls or adapt to suit your baby's appetite.
Texture	Smooth, slightly thicker purées – no need to sieve if using a liquidizer.
Flavours	Begin to offer simple combinations of a food that your baby has tried with something new. Dairy foods and meat can be offered after 6–8 weeks of weaning.*
Vegetables	Try cooked and puréed courgettes (with skins), green beans, mushrooms, cauliflower and broccoli.
Fruit	Introduce ripe raw fruit, such as papaya (all seeds and skin removed), mango, banana and avocado; or fresh apricots or plums that have been cooked and sieved.
Grains and pulses	Mix tiny portions of red lentils puréed with vegetables and a few drops of olive oil for extra energy.
Dairy foods	Full-fat yoghurt, fromage frais or ricotta.*
Meat	Well-cooked chicken or turkey, lean red meat.
Fish	No
Eggs	No
Nuts, seeds	No
Milk	Breast feeds or at least 600ml (20fl oz/1 pint) formula milk.
Drinks	Cooled boiled water.

*Delay introducing these foods if there is a family history of food allergies.

At 6–9 months

Meals per day	Three mini-meals a day; slowly bring timings more in line with meals for the rest of the family.
Portion size	Gradually increase amounts to 3–4 tablespoonfuls, but be guided by your baby.
Texture	Finely mashed; gradually introduce more texture, as your baby is ready, with first finger foods.
Flavours	If weaning is well under way, begin to broaden your baby's diet and offer much more variety; try adding tiny amounts of garlic, mild spices such as coriander, turmeric, cumin and cinnamon as well as fresh or dried herbs.
Vegetables	Stronger-tasting vegetables, such as leeks, spinach, onion, cabbage, fennel, coloured peppers; and those with more fibre, such as sweetcorn or frozen peas. Cooked vegetable finger foods, such as small broccoli florets or carrot sticks, from 8 months.
Fruit	Soaked and cooked dried fruits, small amounts of fresh orange juice* added to meals to boost iron absorption.
Grains and pulses	Gluten grains: wheat, barley, oats; pasta; flour in cooking; millet grains, couscous, semolina; tiny amounts of less fibrous soaked dried beans, such as butter beans; wider choice of lentils. Keep portions small.*
Dairy foods	Cow's milk may now be used in cooking; mild-tasting Cheddar cheese, Edam, low-salt cream cheese or tofu.*
Meat	Widen range of meats. Tiny amounts of well-cooked liver may be included once a week.
Fish	Steamed plaice, sole or trout, cooked and puréed with vegetables and carefully checked for any bones.
Eggs	Well-cooked whole egg, finely chopped.
Nuts, seeds	No
Milk	Breast feeds or at least 500–600ml (17–20fl oz/1 pint) formula or follow-on formula milk.
Drinks	Tap water (no need to boil first).

*Delay these foods if there is a family history of food allergies. Peanuts should only be given to children over 12 months.

At 9–12 months

Meals per day	Three main meals plus one or two healthy snacks.
Portion size	3–6 tablespoonfuls, or be guided by your baby.
Texture	Coarsely mashed or chopped blends; cooked and raw finger foods.
Flavours	Mashed portions of family meals may now be offered, but without added salt or sugar.
Vegetables	Wide range of vegetables, including fresh or canned tomatoes.
Fruit	Fresh fruit juices (see Drinks, below), sieved berry fruits, canned fruit in natural juice.
Grains and pulses	Include small amounts of chickpeas, split peas, kidney and haricot beans; more grains, but limit unrefined grains as fibre content is high.
Dairy foods	Increase amounts, but still avoid blue cheeses and soft French cheeses.
Meat	Gradually increase amounts and choice. Tiny portions of unsmoked low-salt/sodium ham (not bacon, which is too salty) can now be offered.
Fish	Small amounts of oily fish such as salmon, herring, mackerel, sardines (making sure all bones are removed), canned tuna in water. Still avoid giving any shellfish.
Eggs	Well-cooked chopped egg.
Nuts, seeds	Finely ground nut and seed butters made by grinding plain or toasted nuts with sunflower oil or full-fat milk.*
Milk	Breast feeds or 500–600ml (17–20fl oz/1 pint) follow-on formula milk.
Drinks	Fresh fruit juice diluted 1 part juice to 10 parts water with meals, water at other times.

*Delay these foods if there is a family history of food allergies. Peanuts should only be given to children over 12 months.

Did you know?

Research shows that babies who are offered a wide range of foods from 6 months onwards are less likely to be fussy eaters in later life.

From 5 months

(or 4 weeks into weaning)

- New foods to introduce

- Five day menu plan for a
  5-month-old baby

- Hot on hygiene

- The importance of texture

- Can you bring up your baby on a
  vegetarian diet?

3

New foods to introduce

Now that weaning is well under way, you can begin to introduce simple flavour combinations to your baby, and offer more varied fruit and vegetables.

Top: *Keep purées smooth, and gradually begin to make them thicker.*

Bottom: *Try mixing a little cooked broccoli with some potato or parsnip.*

By the time you have reached 4 weeks into weaning, your baby should have settled happily into accepting mini-meals from a spoon, and will probably be eating two meals a day. Adjust the amounts to suit your baby's appetite. No two babies are alike and, just like adults, their appetites vary from day to day or meal to meal. Although your baby is still too little to sit in a highchair, a car baby-seat or adjustable reclining seat will serve as a good interim measure.

Try blending a food that your baby has tried and likes with something new, such as:

- Puréed raw ripe fruits, such as papaya, mango, avocado, melon.
- Cooked and puréed fresh apricots, peaches and plums.
- Small quantities of well-cooked red lentils mixed with carrots or butternut squash.
- Cooked and puréed courgettes, broccoli and cauliflower.
- Their first tiny taste of wholemilk, plain unsweetened yoghurt, fromage frais or ricotta cheese, but only if there is no family history of asthma or eczema.
- Small amounts of well-cooked puréed chicken or turkey. Tiny amounts of red meat can be introduced, but this is quite strong-tasting and difficult to purée until smooth, so you may prefer to wait until your baby is 6 months old.

Nature's convenience foods

While jars of ready-made baby food make an ideal standby, so too do whole fresh fruits.

- **Bananas** have long been a favourite, being easy to mash with a fork, cheap and readily available. Choose ripe bananas – they not only taste sweeter, because the starch in them changes to sugar on ripening, but are easier for a baby to digest, with less chance of painful wind.
- **Melons,** with their mild taste, are also a good choice. Choose orange-fleshed cantaloupe for valuable vitamin C or the pale green Ogen and pale yellow honeydew for their fresh, thirst-quenching taste.
- **Papaya** would be an interesting choice. This exotic fruit is now much more readily available in all supermarkets. It looks a little like a mango but, when cut in half, has a beautiful salmon-pink flesh and jewel-like black seeds. Scoop out the seeds and discard them, along with the skin, then mash or blend the flesh to a smooth purée. The fruit contains the enzyme papain, which is similar to an enzyme found in the digestive system; consequently it is easily broken down by the body, making it ideal for a baby.
- **Mangoes** are a rich source of vitamin A, which is in an easily absorbed form, and vitamin C. As before, choose ripe fruits because they are more easily digested.

tip

Introduce any new food at the mid-morning feed – then, if your baby has a reaction or tummy upset, the symptoms will have settled down by the time you all go to bed.

Above: *Make sure you remove all the seeds before puréeing some melon.*

51

Five-day menu plan for a 5-month-old baby

2–3 meals a day

	Day 1	Day 2	Day 3	Day 4	Day 5
Breakfast	Milk feed	Milk feed	Milk feed	Milk feed	Milk feed
Mid-morning	Broccoli and butternut squash purée	Avocado purée	Banana purée	Courgette purée	Green bean and sweet potato purée
Lunch	Milk feed	Milk feed	Milk feed	Milk feed	Milk feed
Mid-afternoon	Apple purée	Parsnip and apple purée	Carrot and potato purée	Pear purée	Courgette purée
Tea	Milk feed	Milk feed	Milk feed	Milk feed	Milk feed
Bedtime	Milk feed	Milk feed	Milk feed	Milk feed	Milk feed

Remember!

Don't be biased – just because you don't like a certain food or combination, it doesn't follow that your baby will feel the same!

Above right: *Avocados are rich in vitamins and minerals, and make a quick lunch purée that's easy to digest. Do not add lemon juice.*

Hot on hygiene

Cleanliness is vitally important when you are carrying out any food preparation, but it is particularly important when you are cooking for a baby.

- If you have a dishwasher, the steam cycle will sterilize cooking equipment. Otherwise rinse washed pans, large knives, chopping boards, liquidizer goblets or ice-cube trays with boiling water before use (see page 19).
- Rinse root vegetables after preparation to make sure that any soil residues have been removed. Use boiled water from the kettle until your baby is 6 months and tap water after that.
- Use cooled boiled water from the kettle or cooled formula milk to thin finished purées until your baby is 6 months old. After 6 months, use tap water or cow's milk.
- Sterilize bowls and spoons in a steam sterilizer or a cold-water sterilizing unit, or by completely immersing them in simmering water for 5 minutes (see also page 19).

Above: Make sure vegetables are thoroughly washed. For root vegetables, rinse after peeling to make sure there are no soil residues left.

Left: As your baby grows and matures, so purées can become thicker and coarser, moving on to mashed and later chopped foods.

The importance of texture

While it is important to offer foods at the right time, it is equally important to offer foods of the right texture (see box, below). If foods are too thick or lumpy at the beginning, your baby will not be able to swallow them and may be put off eating from a spoon.

tip

The more your baby is allowed to experiment feeding himself, the more adventurous he is likely to be trying new flavours and textures.

As with all things, be guided by your baby. The ages given below are a guide, so do not be tempted to change suddenly from puréeing to chopping just because your baby has moved into the next age range or it will be too much of a shock for him. The key is to change the texture of your baby's food very gradually.

Introducing new textures

• **4–5 months or 1–4 weeks into weaning**
Ultra-smooth sieved purées of baby rice or potato, moving on to cooked puréed apple or pear.

• **5–6 months or 5–8 weeks into weaning**
Smooth purées, slightly thicker and not sieved.

• **6–9 months or 9 weeks into weaning**
Puréed or mashed mixtures with smooth, easy-to-chew lumps. Progress to coarser textures as your baby is ready. Introduce cooked broccoli and cooked carrot sticks as first finger foods.

• **9–12 months or when weaning is well established**
Your baby should now be happy to try coarser textures, with either mashed or finely chopped foods, plus raw and cooked finger foods.

Above: If a baby is given purée that is too sloppy for too long, he may be reluctant to move on to coarser foods.

Can you bring up your baby on a vegetarian diet?

Vegetarianism is now more common, and it is acceptable to bring up a baby on this diet. The basic guidelines are the same: offer small amounts gradually, until a wide range is accepted.

The biggest difference lies in what foods to offer from 5–6 months. Instead of obtaining protein from meat and fish, a vegetarian baby will receive his first protein from dairy foods and red lentils, then mixed grains and eggs, then pulses, larger lentils, finely ground nut and seed butters and soya products (unless he has a known allergy).

Providing sufficient amounts of iron can be a problem. For babies over 6 months, offer puréed dried apricots, small amounts of prune juice, molasses, red lentils, mixed grains and fortified breakfast cereals. Aid iron absorption by serving foods rich in vitamin C, such as chopped tomatoes, green vegetables, a little freshly squeezed orange juice or a fruit dessert. Include plenty of dairy products for vitamin D and calcium, but be sure not to overload your baby's diet with fibre.

A vegan diet, which also excludes dairy products and eggs, is more difficult so if you wish your baby to follow one, you will need to seek advice from a State Registered paediatric dietician to ensure that his diet contains sufficient vitamin B12, vitamin D and calcium.

Above: Dried fruit can be a useful source of iron, if it is served with some vitamin C-rich fresh fruit or vegetables, to aid its absorption.

What about organic foods?

The popularity of organic foods has risen dramatically – but are they as good for us as we are led to believe they are? And are they worth the extra money we need to spend?

tip

If you choose to offer organic foods, make the switch before breastfeeding stops or as weaning begins (when your baby is at her most vulnerable) and try to continue until her immune system is fully developed, at 2 years.

The arguments for organic foods

- They are environmentally friendly.
- They contain higher levels of important minerals and vitamin C.
- They are free of preservatives.
- No chemicals (artificial fertilizers, pesticides, hormones, growth-promoters, antibiotics) are used in their production.
- Animals reared organically are not fed animal-based foodstuffs.
- They are free of genetic modification, whose long-term effects are unknown.

Babies are particularly vulnerable to chemical residues because:

- They have a greater potential exposure to residues than adults because, on a weight-for-weight basis, babies consume more fruit, vegetables, eggs and dairy products.
- A baby's gastrointestinal tract is more easily penetrated so that residues in food are more likely to be absorbed.
- High levels of residues could permanently affect a baby's immune system. For example, routine dosing of animals with antibiotics has been shown to affect human antibiotic resistance.
- Impurities in the mother's food can be transferred to her baby during breastfeeding.

The arguments against organic foods

- They are more expensive. Families who cannot afford them may decide not to buy fruit, vegetables or even dairy foods for their children, which is potentially far more damaging!
- Shopping is more difficult. Organic foods contain no preservatives, so you will have to shop more frequently. Also, it can be difficult to ensure that foods are truly organic (see box, right).

Buying organic foods

To make sure that the food you are buying is truly organic, check that it is certified and labelled with the logo of the Soil Association, Organic Farmers and Growers Ltd, the Organic Food Federation or the UK Register of Organic Food Standards.

Left: Steam-cooking organic vegetables ensures that they retain even more vitamin C for you and your baby.

Making your own baby food

What better start can you give your baby than home-made baby foods made with the freshest and best ingredients? Since they are home-made, you have complete control over all the ingredients used in their preparation.

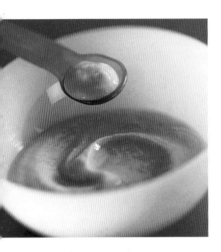

Above: There is much satisfaction to be gained from serving home-cooked baby foods.

Once your baby has enjoyed a few meals of baby rice, you can start to make your own baby food. Sterilizing equipment and preparing food for one mini-meal at a time can be extremely fiddly, so save time and effort by batch-cooking large amounts of single-flavour purées, such as sweet potato, butternut squash, carrot, parsnip, apple or pear purée, and freezing them in the sections of an ice-cube tray. Put the frozen cubes into a sterilized plastic box, seal it, label it with the contents and date of freezing, and store it in the freezer until required. Freezing baby food also means that it is easy to increase the amounts: simply defrost one, two, three or more cubes to suit your baby's growing appetite.

Once your baby has learned to like each new flavour, either mixed with a little baby rice or served on its own, you can begin to vary the menu by mixing different-flavoured cubes together. As your baby matures, make up new baby meals and adjust the texture: mix one cube of smooth baby purée with one that is a little thicker as a gradual introduction to a coarser texture.

Making your own baby food ensures that you know exactly what goes into it. With food that you have prepared yourself, you know that there are no hidden bulking agents, salt or added sugar. Moreover, if you are going back to work, it can be heartening to know that, even if you cannot be with your baby during the day, you are still providing her with the best meals that you can.

Home-made chicken stock

Stock cubes, even those made with reduced salt, are still very strongly flavoured and are unsuitable for a baby. Making your own chicken stock sounds like a job for serious cooks and chefs, but it is very easy – and virtually free because the carcass is usually discarded after the meat has been eaten.

1 Put a chicken carcass into a medium-sized saucepan and cover with 2 litres (3½ pints) of boiling water.

2 Flavour with a thickly sliced carrot and a quartered onion, and perhaps the top of a leek, a stick of celery or a few fresh herbs from the garden.

3 Bring all the ingredients to the boil, half-cover the pan and simmer for 1½ hours or until the liquid is reduced by half.

4 Strain into a bowl, cover and leave to cool. Transfer to the fridge as soon as possible.

5 Use the stock to make your own baby food and freeze it as soon as possible. Alternatively, freeze the stock in small containers, defrost, make into baby food and then use straight away. Do not refreeze home-made stock.

Above: *Even after you have returned to work, you can still serve home-made mini-meals to your baby by batch-cooking and freezing them at the weekend.*

Basic equipment for making baby food

The task of cooking your own baby food can be as high- or as low-maintenance as you care to make it. Baby food can be made by anyone, irrespective of your budget or how much cookery knowledge and experience you have.

Above: Blenders come in a wide range of sizes and prices.

You will probably already have most of the equipment that you will need in your kitchen, with the exception perhaps of a liquidizer, a food-processor or a mouli-mill. Which machine you use to transform a simple baby meal into an ultra-smooth purée is very much up to you.

- **Liquidizers** are generally cheaper than food-processors and are able to purée foods until they are very smooth.
- **Food-processors** are larger and ideal for making larger quantities, but not all types purée foods until ultra-smooth, so you may still need to use a traditional sieve as well.
- **Combination liquidizers and processors** are by far the most flexible – some even come with small spice-mills. They are ideal for chopping or puréeing baby-sized amounts from a family meal, but they are the most expensive option.
- **Electric hand-blenders** can be used to purée food while it is still in the saucepan, although first-stage purées may still need to be pressed through a sieve to make them smooth enough.
- **Hand-held mouli-mills** are rather like a cross between a sieve and a grater, with a wind-up handle that pushes the food through a selection of metal discs, each with a different-sized hole. Straightforward and easy to use, they are rather labour-intensive for large amounts.

- **Sieves and forks** are old-fashioned, cheap and reliable, although very labour-intensive for large amounts.
- **Extras** – as hygiene is essential, you may like to invest in some new chopping boards (keeping one for meat and the other for vegetables), a new cook's knife and perhaps a medium-sized nonstick saucepan. A steamer is also invaluable: look out for stacking steamer and saucepan sets or fold-out stainless-steel steamer baskets that sit in the top of a saucepan. If you plan to do a lot of steaming, electric steamers are also available.

Above: Hand-held mouli-mills are available in all stainless steel or part plastic and part steel, as shown here.

Left: Fold-out stainless steel steamers are ideal for you, if storage space is at a premium.

61

Freezing home-made baby food

While your baby's appetite is small, probably the easiest and most flexible way of freezing purées is in sections of an ice-cube tray. Make sure that the ice-cube trays are sterilized first (see page 19 and 53) and transfer frozen cubes to sterilized plastic boxes. Plastic bags (which cannot be sterilized) can be used after your baby is 6 months old, when sterilizing is no longer needed.

Freezer friends

- Frozen vegetables, such as peas, sweetcorn, broccoli and spinach
- Frozen sliced wholemeal bread and pitta breads
- Frozen cod, haddock, plaice, sole, trout or salmon
- Low-fat, thick-cut oven chips
- Frozen berry fruits

- Make sure that cooked, puréed food is covered and transferred to the fridge as soon as possible.
- Never put warm food in the fridge or freezer.
- Double-check the temperature of your freezer: it should read -18°C (0°F) on a specialist freezer thermometer (these are available from all good hardware shops).
- Fill ice-cube trays with food and transfer when solid to plastic boxes or bags.
- Label all containers of frozen foods with the contents and date of freezing and seal them well.
- Use baby foods within 6 weeks.
- Never refreeze cooked food once it has come out of the freezer and been defrosted.
- Always make sure that food to be defrosted is covered and defrost it either overnight in the fridge or for 2–3 hours at room temperature, transferring it to the fridge when softened.
- Store defrosted baby food in the fridge and use it within 24 hours.

Reheating baby food: microwaving tips

Although most households now have microwave ovens, some professionals still advise against using them for reheating baby food and milk. They are, however, quick and easy to use, and are ideal for baby food.

A microwave oven reheats food quite unlike a conventional oven and, because of this, the outside may feel cool to the touch while the centre is burning hot. These hidden hot-spots could harm your baby, so, if you are using a microwave oven, be sure to stir the food well, or shake any milk, and leave it to stand for 2–3 minutes before serving. Just before giving it to your baby, make sure you stir the food or shake the milk again, and always test the temperature. Do not be tempted to reheat foods until just lukewarm – this is the ideal temperature for bacteria to multiply.

Reheating know-how

- Never reheat foods more than once, even though your baby may only have eaten a tiny amount.
- Make sure ready-made foods are reheated thoroughly until piping hot and then allowed to cool before serving.
- Always stir food well before serving so that the temperature is even.
- Always check the temperature of cooled food before serving to a baby.
- If you are warming milk in a bottle, always be sure to remove the top and teat. Shake it well and test the temperature on the inside of your wrist.

Above: *Hungry babies get impatient waiting for their meals to reheat. A microwave saves time, but make sure you stir food well to avoid hot spots.*

Ready-made meals

Having a young baby is exhausting and, if you are returning to work, you may worry how to fit all the things that need doing into the day. Pure baby rice is the ideal first food especially when the meals are so tiny. As your baby's appetite increases, and the range of food broadens, so too will the range of commercial foods available. Baby cereals, fortified with extra vitamins and minerals, are ideal for a quick breakfast, while jars of baby purée are convenient and a great standby – but try to keep them as a standby rather than the norm.

tip

Buy baby foods that are organic and additive-free and have no added salt, sugar or sweeteners.

Commercially produced baby foods can work out much more expensive than home-prepared foods, and some may contain ingredients that would not be found in home-made foods. Get into the habit of reading labels. If the label on the jar says 'carrot purée', then carrot should be at the top of the list of ingredients, and should not be listed halfway down. (Ingredients are always listed in descending order of proportion.)

Be wary of:
- **Bulking agents**, such as starch, modified starch, cornflour, maltodextrin, rice flour, soya flour, gelatin, pectin and vegetable gums. These are just added as fillers.
- **Sweeteners** – sugar may be listed as sucrose, dextrose, maltose, glucose, corn syrup, inverted sugar, fructose or concentrated fruit juice. Once you begin to study food labels, you may find that more than one of these is included in the list of ingredients. For example, some pots of

flavoured yoghurt and fromage frais that are aimed at young children can often contain up to 4 teaspoonfuls of sugar.

- **Colourings, anti-oxidants, emulsifiers and stabilizers** with an E number.
- **Gluten** – foods for babies under 6 months old should be gluten-free.

Above left: *Bought baby food is a great time-saver. Before you use a jar, always make sure that the seal has not been broken.*

Above right: *Alternate bought baby food with home-made meals.*

From 6 months

(or 8 weeks into weaning)

- New foods to introduce

- Introducing more taste

- How big is a portion?

- Five-day menu plan for a 6-month-old baby

4

- Encouraging your baby to be more adventurous

- Nutritional needs

- Texture: from purées to mash – and beyond

New foods to introduce

At 6 months, the food can be more varied, as your baby's digestive system is now more mature and able to cope with more complex food.

Remember!

Variety is the key to a healthy diet. If your baby starts weaning at 6 months, she will progress to a mixed diet more quickly than a baby who is weaned earlier.

Above: Gluten grains such as pasta can now be introduced.

If your baby's weaning is already well under way, she will be happily tucking into three mini-meals a day. As the amounts increase, so will their nutritional importance; until now, you have just been introducing your baby to the idea of eating from a spoon. At 6 months of age, your baby's natural body store of iron and zinc will be almost used up and it is vital to supply these and other minerals and vitamins in the foods that your baby eats. Protein from meat, fish, poultry and lentils is, of course, vital for growth and development, while dairy products, such as cheese and yoghurt, provide energy in a concentrated form suitable for growing babies.

Your baby's menu can now become much more exciting and varied, and may include a selection of the following:

- Gluten grains, such as wheat, barley, oats and rye, as well as pasta, bread and flour in cooking.
- Full-fat cow's milk may now be used in cooking, or with breakfast cereals, but do not give it as a drink until your baby is at least 1 year old.
- Mild cheeses, such as mild Cheddar, Edam or cream cheese.
- Mashed and well-cooked, whole hard-boiled hen's eggs.
- Increased amounts and types of lean red meat and poultry.
- Tofu – if there is no family history of soya allergy.
- Plaice, sole or trout may be introduced, checking trout carefully for any bones.
- Cooked, soaked dried apricots and other kinds of dried fruit.

- Orange juice – you can now add tiny amounts to cooked dishes.
- Stronger-tasting vegetables, such as leek, onion, spinach, cabbage and coloured peppers, plus more fibrous peas and sweetcorn.
- Tiny amounts of well-cooked liver mixed with vegetables, but do not serve more often than once a week.

New research

1 While it was once thought that babies should be brought up on a mild, quite restricted and bland diet, professionals now feel that the more varied the diet from 6 months onwards the less likelihood there will be of the child developing food fads. As a result, the child's diet will become better and more varied later in life, as he grows into adulthood. Well, that's the theory!

2 Some professionals feel that a baby needs to learn to like new flavours. Many babies reject foods when they are first offered them, just because they are new and strange, yet when the foods are served a second time, after a few days' break, they are received more favourably because they then seem familiar.

3 It is thought that what a mother eats and drinks during pregnancy affects the odour of the amniotic fluid that cushions the baby in the womb. Before birth, babies learn to associate strong flavours, such as garlic, onion and vanilla, with the womb, and they carry this association into childhood and later adulthood.

4 It is also thought by professionals that breast milk may change slightly depending on what the mother has been eating, thus introducing the baby to more flavours and tastes before weaning even begins.

Top: *Adding red peppers to baby food helps to give colour and sweetness, without the acidity associated with tomatoes.*

Bottom: *Fresh or dried herbs add flavour to baby food, but use sparingly so they are not overpowering.*

69

Introducing more taste

Now that your baby is well established in a new style of eating and happily tucking into three meals a day, you can begin to add a little more flavour to her food.

Begin by mixing more ingredients together, adding a little onion or leek to mixed root vegetables, for example. You could add a tiny sprinkling of ground spice – such as cinnamon, nutmeg, turmeric, coriander or cumin – a few fresh herb leaves, or a small sprinkling of dried garlic, even a small slice of fresh garlic for an adventurous baby. Obviously, avoid hot or very strong spices this stage.

Some things to try

- **Baby risotto:** risotto rice + little diced butternut squash + fresh sage leaves.
- **Lamb hotpot:** diced lamb + potato + carrot + fresh rosemary sprigs.
- **Mediterranean chicken:** diced chicken breast + courgettes + red peppers + pasta + basil leaves.
- **First dhal:** red lentils + carrots + pinch of ground turmeric, coriander and cumin.
- **Pumpkin pilaf:** diced pumpkin + millet grain + ground allspice.
- **Plum sundae:** puréed plums + ricotta cheese + ground cinnamon.
- **Peach fool:** puréed peach and apple + yoghurt + ground cardamom.

Top: A first dhal, mashed to a smooth, thick purée – ideal for vegetarian babies.

Bottom: Baby risotto, flecked with golden cubes of butternut squash, then blended to a coarse purée in a food processor.

How big is a portion?

When you first offer solid food, the amount needed is tiny: just 1–2 teaspoonfuls of ground rice mixed with breast milk, formula milk or cooled boiled water as a taster. As your baby, and more importantly her digestive system, learns to cope with solid food, you can increase the amount and number of meals gradually. Introduce a second mini-meal 2–3 weeks into weaning and a third meal 2–3 weeks after that (or 6–9 weeks after weaning first began).

At 6–9 months, your baby will probably be eating 3–4 tablespoonfuls or more of solids two to three times a day. At 9–12 months, she will probably be eating 3 tablespoons of baby cereal for breakfast and 3–6 tablespoonfuls of a savoury baby lunch and dinner, followed by mashed fruit, yoghurt or fromage frais as a pudding at one or two meals, perhaps with one or two tiny healthy snacks. If your baby is happy, sleeping well and gaining weight steadily, continue offering these amounts.

Do not be tempted to encourage your baby to finish off that last spoonful in the bowl. She will soon show you when she has had enough.

Above: A baby's appetite will vary from day to day and meal to meal, in much the same way as an adult's.

Five-day menu plan for a 6-month-old baby

With a baby, an older child and one or more adult meals to cater for, you may sometimes feel a little stuck on what to serve to your baby. The chart below shows a suggested plan to give you some ideas. You might want to mix and match some of the meals, depending on what is in your freezer, and the kind of meals that your baby prefers. You may also find it helpful to make a plan for the following week regularly, and stick it on your fridge door.

	Day 1	Day 2
Breakfast	• Oat-based baby cereal with full-fat cow's milk	• Wheat-based baby cereal with full-fat cow's milk
Mid-morning	• Milk feed	• Milk feed
Lunch	• Steamed trout mashed with potato and broccoli. • Natural yoghurt mixed with dried aprict or apple purée	• Macaroni cheese • Fresh peach purée
Mid-afternoon	• Milk feed	• Milk feed
Tea	• Chopped red pepper, courgette and carrot mashed with cooked pasta	• Sweet potato and carrot purée served with cooked broccoli as finger food
Bedtime	• Milk feed	• Milk feed

Left: *Children's mealtimes seem to come around so quickly – it can help you to organize the day if you know what's on the menu.*

Day 3	Day 4	Day 5
• Oat-based baby cereal with full-fat cow's milk	• Wheat-based baby cereal with full-fat cow's milk	• Oat-based baby cereal with full-fat cow's milk
• Milk feed	• Milk feed	• Milk feed
• Butternut squash and risotto rice • Mashed banana	• Dhal with red lentils, carrots and potato • Cooked apple purée	• Lamb fillet and mixed vegetable and potato casserole • Baby yoghurt
• Milk feed	• Milk feed	• Milk feed
• Well cooked scrambled egg with toast strips as finger food	• Steamed chicken breast and broccoli mashed with rice and served with cooked carrot sticks as finger food	• Mashed avocado with pitta bread fingers
• Milk feed	• Milk feed	• Milk feed

Encouraging your baby to be more adventurous

Babies and young children learn so much from their parents. What we eat as adults can greatly influence our children and it can be hard not to pass on our dislikes for certain foods.

Above: If children see their parents tucking into healthy snacks, they are more likely to do the same.

Introducing your child to a varied and healthy diet can be a good opportunity for you to review what the rest of the family is eating. Combining busy jobs, school runs and daycare for a baby can mean that even the best and most well-intentioned parent quickly falls into a limited food routine, with a supermarket run on automatic pilot that could almost be done blindfolded.

What are you eating?

Try to stand back and take a fresh look at last week's menu.
- Are your meals as healthy as they could be?
- How often do you steam, stir-fry or make salads?
- Do you eat enough portions of fruit and vegetables each day?
- Could you lower the amount of salt in your diet?
- What kind of snacks do you go for: a packet of crisps, a biscuit or an apple?

How are you eating it?

It is not just what food you eat, but the way in which you eat it.
- Do you sit together as a family?
- Do you eat around the TV?
- Do you make mealtimes a social occasion?
Although a baby in a highchair will be unaware of eating as part of a social group, it will not be very long before all the family can eat the same meals together and share in the high and the low points of

the day. Obviously, not everyone can be at home at the same time every day, but perhaps one parent and child can eat together at one meal on most days, or the children can eat together with a parent sitting at the table, even if the parents are not eating until later. If parents do not set an example, how can children learn how to interact at the table? And how can older children realize that there should be more to a meal than a quick refuelling stop between TV shows?

Below: *Interact with your child at mealtimes, offering encouragement and praise when new food is tried.*

Nutritional needs

Vitamins and minerals are essential to your child's health and his needs change with age (see box, page 77, left).

Iron-rich foods

The following foods are particularly rich in iron.

- Green leafy vegetables: broccoli, watercress, spinach, kale, green cabbage, spring greens and frozen peas.
- Dried fruit purées, especially apricots.
- Whole grains such as millet and amaranth (a grain that looks like wheatgerm).
- Red lentils, moving on to dried beans and then other larger lentils.
- Iron-fortified baby breakfast cereals.
- Well-cooked egg yolk.
- Chicken and turkey.
- Fish.

Should you give your child vitamin drops?

Some health authorities recommend that babies have vitamin drops from the age of 6 months upwards if they are breastfed, or from the age of 1 to 5 years if they are bottle-fed. Fortified with vitamins A, C and D, these drops act as a nutritional safety net and are particularly important for babies who are:

- Breastfed.
- Receiving less than 500ml (17fl oz) infant formula or follow-on milk.
- Following a vegetarian diet.
- Late weaning.
- Fussy eaters.
- Getting little exposure to sunlight.

Toddlers and older children who enjoy a mixed and varied diet may not need vitamin drops. If you are concerned, get your child's weight checked regularly and talk to your health visitor or doctor.

Why your baby needs iron

Iron is needed by the body for brain development, to help build up resistance to infection and to transport oxygen around the body via the bloodstream. By the age of 6 months, the iron stores with which your baby was born will have begun to run out and you will need to supply iron in the foods that you offer. At this early stage, your baby will probably not be eating much red meat (one of the best sources of iron), so be sure to include plenty of iron-rich foods in his diet (see box, left).

Why your baby needs zinc

A baby is born with a body store of zinc, which, like iron, is used up by around 6 months of age. Zinc is vital for maintaining and replicating each individual's genetic material (DNA) and is also important for normal growth, efficient functioning of the immune system and the development of the ovaries and testes in childhood. It is found in meat, poultry, dairy foods, eggs and cereals, although zinc from cereals is more difficult for the body to absorb. Vegetarians and vegans (see page 55) may need zinc supplements.

Your baby's changing daily nutritional needs

- **4–5 months**

Milk is still providing all your baby's nutrition. At this stage, introduce the idea of eating solids from a spoon.

- **5–6 months**

Milk still supplies the bulk of your baby's nutritional needs. Fruit and vegetables are starting to provide energy, vitamins and minerals.

- **6–9 months**

Food now needs to provide the bulk of your baby's nutrition. Iron and zinc are important because your baby's body store has now been used up. Include two portions of fruit and/or vegetables.

- **9–12 months**

Try to include three to four mini-servings of fruit and vegetables, served as fruit juice or cooked. One mini-serving of starchy foods per meal – breakfast cereal, rice, potato or pasta. Two protein foods: meat, fish, eggs, lentils, cheese or tofu.

How to increase iron absorption

Eating foods rich in vitamin C greatly increases the body's ability to absorb iron from iron-rich foods. Such foods include mango, papaya or kiwi fruit, perhaps served as a pudding. Or add a little orange juice or finely diced tomato to a savoury dish at the end of cooking, or serve the main course with a green leafy vegetable.

Texture: from purées to mash – and beyond

Once your baby is happy and used to smooth mashed meals, begin to make the mash a little thicker and coarser. If your baby is happy to make this transition, build up to very finely chopped meals. If you have a food-processor or a liquidizer, simply run the motor for a shorter time. If you use a mouli-mill, change the disc to one with slightly larger holes.

Does your baby hate lumps?

Some babies are reluctant to move away from a comfortingly smooth baby purée to a coarser one and can become quite distressed, appearing to gag on their food, even when the lumps are soft. Try not to over-react and do not lift your baby out of her chair the moment that she looks slightly agitated. Soothing words and body signals should quickly reassure her, although, as always, be guided by your baby. Slowly introduce her to foods with more texture, at first choosing very soft lumps of fruit or vegetables that are easy to chew. It may help to mix some smooth puréed cubes of baby food with a cube of food that has more texture.

Left: Add texture to your child's diet by encouraging him to eat some cooked pieces of fruit and vegetables, or toast fingers.

First finger foods

As your baby's hand-to-eye coordination improves, you will find that she will start to put everything into her mouth. At this stage you could introduce some first finger foods, putting them straight onto the table of the highchair. Much of what you offer will get squashed and be dropped on the floor but, with practice, your baby will become more adept at this new and tricky skill.

You can choose from the following:

- Just-cooked broccoli or cauliflower florets.
- Cooked carrot sticks.
- A tablespoonful or two of cooked frozen mixed vegetables.
- Miniature breadsticks.
- Toast fingers.
- Cooked pasta shapes.

Remember!

Never leave a baby unattended while eating, especially when she is feeding herself!

Left: Don't worry too much about table manners at this stage. Enjoyment of a meal is more important.

From 9 to 12 months

- New foods to introduce

- Changing textures

- Is fresh always best?

- Growing independence

- Five-day menu plan for a
  9–12-month-old baby

5

- Eating with the family

- Fussy eaters

- What to aim for

- Is your baby getting the right nutrients?

New foods to introduce

Your baby has come a long way in just 4 or 5 months and the days of ultra-smooth first purées are long gone. He will now be eating a broad and varied diet, trying to feed himself and almost ready to share family meals.

Above: Encourage your baby now to eat food that is coarsely mashed or finely chopped.

New foods to include are:
- Raw fruit and vegetable finger foods.
- Mashed portions of the family meal, providing that no sugar or salt is added.
- Fresh fruit juice, diluted by measuring 1 part juice to 10 parts water.
- Well-cooked whole egg, mashed or finely chopped.
- Finely ground nut or seed butters, if there is no history of allergies.
- Tiny portions of oily fish, such as salmon, making sure all bones are removed.
- Canned tuna in water – avoid brine because it will be too salty.
- Fresh or canned tomatoes.
- Tiny amounts of unsmoked low-salt/sodium ham.

As a reminder, the following should still be avoided:
- Salty, sugary or fatty foods.
- Whole or chopped nuts.
- Soft ripened cheese, such as Brie and Camembert.
- Blue cheeses.
- Smoked or salted fish.
- Smoked or unsmoked bacon.
- Paté.
- Liver more than once a week.
- Strong, hot spices, such as chilli.
- Fizzy drinks.
- Tea or coffee.

Changing textures

A recent study suggests that if a baby is not introduced to new textures and tastes until he's 10 months or older, he is more likely to be a fussy or difficult eater when he is a toddler.

Try to encourage your baby gradually away from finely mashed meals to meals that are coarsely mashed or chopped. He will now have some teeth and, combined with strong gums, this may make him quite adventurous. For babies with teething problems, you may find that you almost go backwards. If this is the case, keep baby meals of the texture with which your baby is happiest, but encourage more finger foods so that he is still learning to bite and chew. As always, go at your baby's pace and never force-feed him.

There are a number of ways to introduce more texture to your baby's food:

- Offer more finger foods.
- Put a little grated cheese straight on to the highchair table.
- Stir some soaked couscous, some tiny soup pasta or some cooked rice into a finely mashed or puréed baby meal.
- Mix finely chopped cooked vegetables into some smooth, cheesy polenta.
- Mix some finely chopped melon into some smooth, sieved raspberry or strawberry purée.

Remember!

Do not give your child whole grapes because she may choke on them.

What to do if your child chokes

When a baby begins to feed himself, he can often forget to chew and swallow. For 99 per cent of the time, excess food can be removed from his mouth easily, but occasionally, drastic measures may be needed quickly.

1 Don't waste time trying to remove food from your baby's mouth, unless it can be done easily.

2 Turn your baby face down, supporting his chest with your forearm, and slap firmly with your other hand between his shoulder blades.

3 If this does not work, quickly try again.

4 Ring the emergency services immediately.

Is fresh always best?

Fresh foods may be best, but it is not practical to shop every day, or even two or three times a week, if you have a young family. A well-stocked freezer and store cupboard (see box, below) can be a lifesaver and may also work out cheaper.

Longlife foods for the store cupboard

- Jars of passata, cans of tomatoes
- Low-sugar, low-salt canned baked beans or other pulses
- Canned fruit, preferably in natural juice rather than high-sugar syrups
- Canned fish in water or oil – avoid brine as it is too salty for young children – such as tuna, salmon, sardines
- Dried fruits, such as apricots, dates, sultanas
- Pasta, rice, couscous, millet or polenta
- Dried beans, lentils
- Rice cakes and breadsticks

Standby meals

Handy store-cupboard meals include:
- **Jacket potato** – soft potato filling scooped out and mashed with low-salt/low-sugar baked beans, just-cooked frozen mixed vegetables and grated cheese.
- **Beans on toast** – low-salt/low-sugar baked beans topped with grated cheese and served with toast and carrot fingers.
- **Eggy bread** – sliced bread dipped into beaten egg, fried in a tiny amount of oil and served cut into strips with apple slices.
- **Mini-tortilla** – diced cooked potato, fried in a little oil with finely chopped onion, then topped with frozen mixed vegetables and beaten egg. Cook until the eggs are thoroughly set then cut into strips.
- **Speedy pasta** – frozen mixed vegetables simmered with a little passata then puréed and mixed with just-cooked pasta and grated cheese.
- **Macaroni cheese** – cooked macaroni or other small pasta mixed with cheese sauce and frozen mixed vegetables or well-drained frozen spinach.

Growing independence

As your baby grows, you will discover how keen she is to feed herself. Encourage her: the more she practises the better.

Try not to worry about the mess too much – just have a damp cloth at the ready, to wipe her sticky hands and face with.

1 Give your baby a spoon and a small amount of food in a bowl while you feed her the main part of the meal from a separate bowl and spoon. If she refuses to let you feed her, let her try to feed herself. Also offer plenty of finger foods (see box, right).

2 Protect the floor, especially if it is carpeted, with a large sheet of plastic so that you need not worry about the mess.

3 Protect your baby's clothes with a plastic bib with sleeves.

4 Use a pelican bib so that your baby can retrieve dropped food.

5 Make sure your baby is strapped into her highchair, so that she cannot climb out when she has had enough.

tip

Boost your child's flagging energy levels with small healthy snacks.

More finger foods

- Halved rice cakes
- Cheese straws
- Mini-sandwiches cut into fingers
- Sliced apple, pear or melon
- Peeled banana
- Slices of raw mushroom
- Raw carrot, celery or cucumber sticks
- Strips of pitta bread, either plain or spread with humous
- Pieces of sliced and cooked lean cocktail sausages
- Diced Cheddar cheese
- Sultanas or raisins

Five-day menu plan for a 9–12-month-old baby

Your baby has learned such a lot in five months. Meals now resemble simple, scaled-down versions of family suppers, and it won't be long before she is joining in with the rest of the family.

	Day 1	Day 2
Breakfast	• Wheat-based baby cereal with full-fat cow's milk	• Oat-based baby cereal with full-fat cow's milk
Mid-morning	• Milk feed	• Milk feed.
Lunch	• Macaroni cheese with frozen spinach added • Mashed or chopped papaya for pudding • Water to drink	• Cheese on toast, cut into tiny squares and served with raw carrot sticks • Chopped slice of melon for pudding • Water to drink
Mid-afternoon	• Milk feed	• Milk feed
Tea	• Miniature ham sandwiches • Slices of ripe pear • Diluted orange juice to drink	• Lamb casserole and mixed root vegetables, mashed and served with couscous • Mashed or chopped strawberries served plain or stirred into fromage frais for the pudding • Water to drink
Bedtime	• Milk feed	• Milk feed

Left: *At 9 to 12 months, it won't be long before your baby is joining in with family meals.*

Day 3	Day 4	Day 5
• Wheat-based baby cereal with full-fat cow's milk	• Oat-based baby cereal with full-fat cow's milk	• Wheat-based baby cereal with full-fat cow's milk
• Milk feed	• Milk feed	• Milk feed
• Courgettes, carrots and peppers cooked with canned tomatoes, with pasta and grated cheese • Fingers of ripe pear • Water to drink	• Chicken risotto with diced butternut squash • Banana as finger food • Water to drink	• Family shepherd's pie with frozen peas • Mashed banana with fromage frais • Water to drink
• Milk feed	• Milk feed	• Milk feed
• Well cooked boiled egg with toast fingers • Cooked dried apricots mixed with natural yoghurt • Water to drink	• Baked beans mashed with grated cheese and served with toast fingers • Diluted apple juice to drink	• Miniature tuna sandwiches • Diced dried fruits, raw carrot sticks • Diluted orange juice to drink
• Milk feed	• Milk feed	• Milk feed

Eating with the family

The first meal that your baby is truly able to share with older members of the family is an important milestone in his development. You may find it easier to offer him some cooked vegetables that he can eat as finger food while you begin your own meal, then offer a finely chopped version of the family meal once you have had a few mouthfuls. Although your baby is now eating a wide range of foods, there are still some important things to remember (see box, page 89).

'I'm hungry!'

As children's appetites are small, it is important to serve meals at regular intervals throughout the day, and to give one or two tiny healthy snacks to boost energy levels in between.

Three-way-stretch suppers: some ideas

Once your baby is joining in with family meals, it is not practical to make different meals for everyone. It is much better to prepare one meal and take out a portion for the baby, another for the toddler, and then to jazz-up the remainder for the adults. Below are some ideas for doing just that.

Chilli con carne

Make up a basic mince mixture flavoured with onion, a can of tomatoes, tomato purée, diced carrot and red pepper, and casserole until tender.
For the baby: Take out a little and process or chop with plain cooked rice.
For the toddler: Spoon a little onto a plate with some plain cooked rice.
For the adults: Add a small can of red kidney beans and chilli sauce. Top with soured cream, diced red onion and sprigs of fresh coriander. Serve with rice and a salad.

Beef Bourguignon

Make up a simple beef casserole.

For the baby: Purée or chop with cabbage and some potato.

For the toddler: Spoon a little onto a plate with some steamed green cabbage and mashed potato.

For the adults: Stir garlic purée, red wine and seasoning into remainder. Serve with cabbage, tossed with butter and caraway seeds, and mashed potato with chopped chives.

Pasta with tomato sauce

Make up a simple tomato sauce, with chopped and fried onion, diced carrot, red peppers, celery and courgettes, flavoured with a little garlic and a can of tomatoes.

For the baby: Purée, mix with chopped pasta. Sprinkle with a little grated Cheddar cheese.

For the toddler: Purée and mix with plain pasta. Sprinkle with a little grated Cheddar cheese.

For the adults: Add extra garlic, pesto or fresh basil, black olives, seasoning and Parmesan cheese.

Mediterranean chicken

Divide chicken thighs or drumsticks, thickly sliced courgettes, red peppers and butternut squash between two roasting tins, one for the toddler and baby, the other for the adults. Add whole garlic cloves, rosemary and coarse sea salt to the adult's tin. Drizzle both with a little olive oil and roast until they are golden.

For the baby: Finely chop or mash a portion, taking meat off the bone and mixing with a little milk or home-made stock if necessary.

For the toddler: Serve a drumstick for him to pick up and eat with some of the vegetables.

For the adults: Drizzle portions with a little balsamic vinegar before serving.

Remember!

- Do not add any salt to the food until your baby has been served.

- Avoid salty stock cubes and make your own stock where possible.

- Keep soy sauce, Worcestershire sauce, chilli and other strong flavours off the children's menu.

- Sweeten puddings with naturally sweet fruits rather than sugar.

- Avoid foods with artificial sweeteners, such as aspartame.

- Always check the temperature of food before serving it to a baby. Quickly cool cooked vegetables by putting them in a sieve and rinsing with cold water.

Fussy eaters

Nearly every child goes through a fussy-eating stage. With a very young child it may be a sign of impending illness, or the result of painful new teeth and sore gums. Older children quickly learn that throwing their food on the floor or playing with it, rather than eating it, provokes a response from the adult.

1 Remember that no child will starve herself if there is food available.

2 Remember that food fads do not last forever – it just feels that way!

3 Keep a food diary. Although your child's diet may not be very varied, you may find that she is eating more yoghurts, bananas or apples than you thought. You may also find that you are offering too many snacks or milky drinks.

4 Talk to other parents. Problems never seem so bad when shared. You may also learn some new survival tactics!

5 Keep calm and take uneaten meals away without a fuss.

6 Look at mealtimes objectively. Does the telephone always ring at the wrong moment? Is your child too tired to eat?

7 Get your child weighed regularly so that any dip in weight can be detected.

8 Ask your doctor or health visitor for advice – there may be a medical reason for him refusing to eat his food.

What to aim for

Carbohydrates

Work up to three or four portions a day by 12 months.

- Cereals, etc: Bread, baby breakfast cereals, pasta.
- Grains: rice, oats, barley, rye, corn and millet.
- Vegetables: pulses, potato, sweet potato, parsnip, plantains, yam.

Fruit and vegetables

Choose fresh or frozen fruit and vegetables, and fruit canned in natural juice. Work up to three or four portions a day by 12 months.

- Carrots, swede, sweetcorn, pumpkin, butternut squash, coloured peppers and mushrooms.
- Green vegetables.
- Orchard fruits: apples, pears, plums, peaches, apricots.
- Berry fruits: strawberries, raspberries, blueberries, red and black currants.
- Exotic fruits: kiwi fruit, oranges, mangoes, papaya, grapes (halved) and melon.

Protein-rich foods

Work up to two servings of milk or other dairy foods and two servings of other protein foods by 12 months.

- Dairy and soya products: milk, cheeses (not blue or unpasteurized), fromage frais, yoghurt, soya milk, tofu.
- Nuts: hazelnuts, cashews, brazil nuts, chestnuts, pine nuts, peanuts, all finely ground (only if there is no family history of allergies).
- Seeds: sunflower, sesame, pumpkin, linseed, all finely ground (only if no family history of allergies).
- Pulses: peas, beans, lentils, quinoa.
- Eggs
- Fish, poultry, red meat and tiny amounts of liver.

Fats and sugars
Use these sparingly.

- Fats: butter, olive oil, seed and nut oils, unhydrogenated margarines.
- Sugars: white and brown sugars, cakes, biscuits, sweets.

Is your baby getting the right nutrients?

If you follow the top ten tips listed below, you can be confident that your baby is getting the right nutrients.

Above: Try to avoid adding sugar of any kind to food for children who are less than a year old.

Top ten tips

1 Variety is the key to a healthy diet. Children offered a wide range of different foods from the age of 6 months are said to be less likely to become fussy eaters in later life.

2 Babies and young children have quite different nutritional needs from adults. Because their growth rate is high but their appetites small, foods need to be nutritionally dense.

3 Naturally occurring fat from wholemilk, cheese and other full-fat dairy food provides concentrated energy in a form easily used by the body, plus fat-soluble vitamins A and D. Revitalize a tired child with a miniature cheese sandwich, warm milky drink or diced cheese and sliced apple.

4 Do not reserve fruit and vegetable for lunch and supper. Offer sliced fruits or raw vegetable sticks as a healthy snack between meals or slice, dice or mash them and add to breakfast cereals. Vitamin C cannot be stored by the body, so it is important to give your child plenty of fruit and vegetables every day.

5 Try to vary the grains in your baby's diet and include a small portion with every meal. Offer a variety and do not rely on wheat only for breakfast cereals, sandwiches and pasta. Offer porridge, rice cakes instead of bread at lunch, and rice, couscous or millet in place of pasta. Too much of one food may run the risk of a food intolerance.

6 Fibre is important for healthy bowels, but do not overload your baby's digestive system or important vitamins and minerals will be flushed straight out of his body before they can be absorbed. Offer foods containing soluble fibre, such as fruits, vegetables and oats, then move on to brown rice, dried pulses and lentils when weaning is well established.

7 Avoid adding sugar to food for children who are less than 1 year old – mix naturally sweet fruits with some sharper ones as a sugar alternative. For older children, keep sweets as a special treat and only offer after a meal. The saliva that is produced during the meal will help to neutralize any remaining sugar on the tooth enamel, thus reducing the chance of tooth decay.

8 Children grow at such a rate that they actually need more protein in relation to their body weight than adults.

9 Look at the way you cook. The water-soluble vitamins B and C are lost in cooking waters, so steam food wherever possible, or use the cooking liquid in gravies and soups. To retain those heat-sensitive vitamins, keep cooking times to the minimum: stir-fry, steam or microwave or offer raw vegetables as finger foods.

10 Offer plenty of water between meals, diluted fruit juices with meals and avoid squashes or fruit cordials if possible.

Top: *Protein-rich food includes nuts, lentils, tofu, dairy produce, pulses and eggs, plus fish, poultry and red meat.*

Bottom: *Lentils and other pulses come in all shapes and sizes.*

Index

An Hachette Livre UK Company
www.hachettelivre.co.uk

A Pyramid Paperback

First published in Great Britain in 2003
by Hamlyn, a division of
Octopus Publishing Group Ltd
2–4 Heron Quays, London E14 4JP
www.octopusbooks.co.uk

Updated in 2006

This revised edition published in 2008

Copyright © Octopus Publishing Group
Limited 2003, 2006, 2008

Sara Lewis asserts the moral right to be
identified as the author of this work.

This material was previously published as
Weaning and First Foods

ISBN 978-0-600-61763-1

A CIP catalogue record for this book is
available from the British Library

Printed and bound in China

10 9 8 7 6 5 4 3 2 1

About the author

Sara Lewis was the cookery editor for *Practical Parenting*
magazine for 12 years. She has a daughter, Alice, and a
son, William, who is vegetarian, so she knows the joys
and frustrations of cooking for children with different
tastes. She also writes regularly for women's magazines
and has written numerous cookery books.

Picture credits

Bubbles/Angela Hampton 18
/Frans Rombout 12
Corbis UK Ltd/Tom Stewart 71
Octopus Publishing Group Limited 42/Stephen
Conroy 51, 52, 53 centre right
/Jeremy Hopley 69 bottom, 92
/David Jordan 14, 19, 20, 28, 32 top left, 32 bottom right,
34, 35, 36, 37 top right, 37 bottom left, 50 top, 50 bottom,
53 bottom left, 54, 55, 57, 58, 60, 61 top right, 61 bottom
left, 65 centre right, 68, 69 top, 70 top, 70 bottom left, 82,
93 top, 93 bottom right
/Peter Pugh-Cook 1, 2, 6, 10, 11, 13, 16, 17, 22, 26, 29,
30, 31, 31 top left, 38, 39, 43, 45, 59, 63, 65 left, 73, 75,
78, 79, 87
/Gareth Sambidge 74

Acknowledgements

I would like to thank Annette Maloney, Health Visitor, for
acting as consultant, and the Department of Health for
their help and advice.
I dedicate this book to my two children, Alice and William.

Executive Editor: Jane McIntosh
Editors: Abi Rowsell and Joss Waterfall
Executive Art Editor: Joanna Bennett
Designer: Ginny Zeal
Production Controller: Louise Hall